BRIGHT TRAVELLERS

BRIGHT TRAVELLERS

Fiona Benson

for Christine, a gift from Sheila!
('Poem for James' sort of
rhymes ...)
with love,
fiona benson xx

CAPE POETRY

Published by Jonathan Cape 2014

4 6 8 10 9 7 5 3

Copyright © Fiona Benson 2014

Fiona Benson has asserted her right under the Copyright, Designs
and Patents Act 1988 to be identified as the author of this work

First published in Great Britain in 2014 by
Jonathan Cape
Random House, 20 Vauxhall Bridge Road,
London SW1V 2SA

www.randomhouse.co.uk

Addresses for companies within The Random House Group Limited can be found at:
www.randomhouse.co.uk/offices.htm

The Random House Group Limited Reg. No. 954009

A CIP catalogue record for this book is available from the British Library

ISBN 9780224099493

The Random House Group Limited supports The Forest Stewardship Council ®
(FSC®), the leading international forest-certification organisation. Our books
carrying the FSC label are printed on FSC®-certified paper. FSC is the only
forest-certification scheme supported by the leading environmental organisations,
including Greenpeace. Our paper procurement policy can be found at
www.randomhouse.co.uk/environment

Typeset by Palimpsest Book Production Ltd,
Falkirk, Stirlingshire

Printed and bound by
CPI Group (UK) Ltd, Croydon CR0 4YY

This book is dedicated to David-Antoine Williams,
with thanks for all his years of careful reading and criticism,
and to my husband James Meredith
and our daughter Isla with all my love

CONTENTS

BRIGHT TRAVELLERS

CAVEAT

But consider the cactus:
its thick hide
and parched aspect

still harbour a moist heart;
nick its rind, and sap
wells up like sugared milk

from the store of water
held beneath its spines,
its armoury of barbs.

And, once a lifetime,
when the slant rains fall
there is this halo of flowers.

DUMNONIA

SUBMERGED FOREST

I wanted the woods
and the woods' corollary –
squirrel hoard,
seeding of teeth,

stag-antler, microlith –
but, when the tide draws back
to its lowest ebb,
all that's left

of the waterlogged forest –
its shoals of acorn
and drifts of leaf,
the shut-up cist of an egg –

are these dank, eroded beds
of peat-stained oak, pocked
with vanished colonies of whelk
and halfway troughed in sand.

How will I get beyond
the let down of these stubs,
how will I find my way back
to the woods,

its dim snares and drowned roots,
the ghost of an owl
still sharking in the treetops,
circling its flooded roost?

CAVE BEAR

You snarl in the lintel
and hold your ground,
your lower jaw blown out,
the roof of your mouth
vented and rough,

constellate
of bone-shard, tooth.
Set at your neck
is the muzzle of a cub,
its crooked skull.

Four hundred thousand years
embedded in this cave:
drip of lime,
dirt in the trench
of your rotted tongue,

the hollow of your brain
cased in stone
till you are a vault
for the one clear thought
of your life:

the cub is dead.
You show your teeth
as the massive slab
of your heart
gives way.

CLAPPER BRIDGE

Clappers: quarried flats
laid like table-boards
over stacked supports,
colonised by lichens, moss.

You love the coppery run
of the stream, its scatter of insects
ringed in brightness
the single, slate-finned fish

but what you want
is the way light plays
on the underside of each granite slab
with a soft, ravelling mobility;

what you want is water-light,
that dance, that luminous flux
and the fraction's shift
in the bedrock of the moor

that puts you on course
with the barrow-builders
shouldering along the lych way,
heavy-footed at the fording place.

URN-BURIAL

A dozen jars, furred
with dirt, a piece of slate
across each throat

and thought, at first,
to be set for resonance,
a slight and subtle antiphon.

But what of this residue,
this rosin,
these thin hearts sleeping,

each occulted in a separate vase?
We slid them back unmarked.
Confess their pulse

in the unstill walls of the church
and you make room for the exiled dead,
crusaders buried abroad,

their quarried hearts
sent home to roost,
like the martins stowed

in their own dull jars
of spit and mud,
querulous under the roof.

ROUGEMONT

for Temperance Lloyd

Next time I'll walk the old cart route to the drop.
For now it's enough to see the castle walls
grown derelict with trees, and the fosse dammed up
with leaves. The fort's long gone, but the gatehouse
squats on still, red-bricked sentry of the city road.
You were brought through this gate for trial.
Now it's nailed across with a mock portcullis
and the doves are frightened from the courtyards and towers
by plastic decoys of owls that spin above the ramparts,
and which I take at first for heads.
My heart is a sad swinging in its cage.
You are a thin thought turning over the walls
in a grey wind, transparent, spider-weight.
I'd have you angry and impenitent and brave.
I'd have you fly from the drop in the shape of a rook,
its rag-and-bone, its bloodshot eye. Instead
you're this palsied old woman in a stained shift
and shawl, your hair thin as carded wool,
hugging your breasts in the cold. On trial
you swore you'd been a cat, that a demon sucked
your private parts, that you pricked and harmed
that man's sick wife. Now you miss the chase
of the Bideford coast but are pleased overall
to be looked at, riding in this cart, when all
your life you've been invisible and walked.

DEVONPORT

Holstered in the Tamar
the low-slung bolts
of submarines come home.

Each breached hood
looks like part of the wharf –
black pontoon or tidal berth

and breathes no word
of its underwater heft,
its airlocks and vaults,

its sintered, nuclear core.
Pray for our fathers on leave
who, in the unstable crucibles

of sleep, crawl
through drowning rooms
of war and sorrow.

Pray for the difficult undoing
of each shining, fissioned load,
the slow decay of isotopes.

Would that the old wars were done with.
The sea is still a torpedo-path,
an Armageddon road.

EMMAUS

And if you should forget
walk out across the Hungerford Bridge
where the city falls back

and pylons loom in the dark
like an avenue of silver birch.
Regard the work:

a simple stitch, it heals
the breach of the river, allows passage and pause
to acknowledge our place

beneath this infinite sky
in a wind that knows we are mortal, porous,
a beautiful trick of the light.

LOVE-LETTER TO VINCENT

'We can paint an *atom* of chaos. A horse, a portrait,
your grandmother, apples, a landscape.'
Vincent Van Gogh (letter 655)

YELLOW ROOM AT ARLES

I was back in your yellow room at Arles –
an ochre cube with a bed like a crib
and your paintings all over the walls . . .
But that's not it. I wanted to tell you
that it's so much worse, that the times
of clarity and grace are more and more
remote, that I'm losing ground to the dark.
So I've dug my way back to your golden room,
your wounded girl, your damned and lovely prostitute,
come to sleep it out, teepeed in your scarlet blanket,
with the lamplight dimmed to a red bordello warmth
and a chair against the door. We'll talk or fuck,
or sit and flip cards, whatever you want,
just ferry me through unharmed, uncut.

STILL LIFE WITH RED HERRING

In Paris you spend too much time
with the whores, tailing them in bars
able to afford only the briefest touch
in the bleak back alley, in the freezing yard.
You hear they finger each other in the dark,
use their tongues, raise sounds that are low and rough,
and utterly ungovernable.

One day you wake – phlegm in your throat,
the shakes – and paint these parched and stinking fish;
here's all you think you know of whores –
the labial gleam of scales,
their gills' slashed silk, their lice.
I'm bored with your disgust.
I've seen the way you look at men,

besides, wouldn't you rather be a woman
raising herself to another woman's lips
like this, like this?

SPRIG OF ALMOND BLOSSOM
IN A GLASS

The orchard will be flying soon,
       every cup ministered to
            by hoverflies
         and bees.

Imagine if their flight-paths shone
       and you could paint the filigree
            of that fine attention,
         its fingering.

This broken sprig drinks from your glass
       its one clear sip and waits
            for the precarious caress
         of your looking –

its shadows and showers, its quick-lit piercing.
       You drew me once. I took
            my widow's mite,
         its passing.

PEAR TREE IN BLOSSOM

This week you paint the slender little pear tree –
or *poirier blanc*, as I must learn to say –
in a mania for orchards. You bind your hands
to keep them warm and peg your easel down
in the rude mistral, but we're striking clear of winter,
taking early mouthfuls of sharp, bright air
and your blood runs clean. Nothing to do but paint,
then sleep, cold as a saint in your hostel bed.

I wonder now how long you'll keep this up –
not the abstinence exactly, but the work –
tree after tree after tree, your dozen orchards blazing,
as if you'd nail down spring; and if you'll stay
to walk down orchard avenues at dusk,
pear in your mouth, your mouth sweet to kiss,
your sticky beard . . . Christ. I never thought I'd beg.
No matter. Here is your *poirier blanc*,
its blossom shining in the dark yard;
here, whatever sorrow waits for us, is hope.

SUNFLOWERS

Look at the millstream mechanism of each throat,
its supple, gulping stem; small hairs
lift the tender raisings of stamen,
and at its centre is a dusting of crumbs.
Still there is this unslaked thirst in the higher cells
as water burns from leaves like shallow pans
and the chaffy head erupts in flames.

Dear one, I listen to you move in the other room
and I burn; your meanest tread outside my door
and I almost come, but you never enter in.
Let me speak to you in signs: here is a seed for your palm.
Each striped seed holds the germ of a flame –
at the heart of each seed this blaze, at the heart of each blaze
a pincushion tucked with seed; and I burn.

SUNFLOWERS

All along I've missed the point
which is the blazing candour of the light,
this pane of yellow paint
set like an open window
on the brightest morning of July.

Against it, the flowers
are a long singing summer in a vase-
farmer's acre, your heart's pure rapture –
just look at the joy in this frame –
meadow-yellow, meadow-green –

most of us are not this brave
our whole damn lives;
teach me to admit
a touch more light.

STARRY NIGHT

you're done with your painting but still
the stars won't keep to their spheres
and the moon blurs

and the black tips of the cypress
and the steel-blue tip of the spire
stir and stir

you're drawn between Catherine Wheel and scourge –
the stars' ecstatic fires –
to the flood

a vertiginous dark which is never
done with you, old pal,
oh it would love you in its weir pond
its drowning well

PORTRAIT WITH A BANDAGED EAR

You show up at my door weeping, exhausted,
a rag tied under your chin like a corpse,
mumbling *chérie, chérie*. I draw you a bath,
soak your dirty underclothes, heat soup.
You sit by the fire in my mother's old housecoat
and doze. When you wake you've turned.
You tell me I stink, open every window to the wind,
throw water all over the bed as if our old love
burned, shout *whore, whore, whore* as you leave.

You show up at my door, drunk but lucid,
your right ear healed to pearly pink buds,
the naked hole in your head flecked with wax.
You eat stew right out of the pan and keep me informed:
mannequins talk filth, they are hungry and bored,
they would like to be saved; birds ventriloquise the damned,
sins that make you muffle your head and shake.
You say you'd like to be well. You shove bread
in your pockets for later and walk back into the cold.

You show up at my door. The veins stand out
on your temples, your nose is pinched and thin.
Angels have voices that spin and shine
and must be listened to side-on; these window-box
geraniums, for instance, spilling crimson petals
on the road, are a counsel for bloodletting, leeches –
you'll interpret their signs for the world. Oh you choose them
over me then come stumbling home, three toes
lost to frostbite, a crust of blood on your upper lip

and I let you in and I let you in and I let you in –
remember the long afternoons of our youth
spent wrapped in the covers as if night would never come,
how fierce you were and clear, back then.

Now I find you stirring in the chamber pot for signs,
or stood in the kitchen, your bare blue limbs shining,
looking for knives. *Chéri, chéri,* we're running
out of grace. Men will come and ask me to confirm
your name. I want you strong and well. Please stay.

IRISES

Much has been made of this single, white iris
as if it meant you, an albino iris
alone amongst the blues, the flower
that didn't fit in. I think instead
you came to the reckoning that you
were everyday, obscene, a run-of-the-mill
blue iris; and never mind that this blue
is the blue of seraphim, or a hot sky
the swallows plumb, sculling headlong
into ordinary joy. You wanted
to be the Messiah. You wanted to open a gap
in the world, to harrow every private hell
and make the heart stand still until it apprehended,
trembling, grace. But each day flares and falls,
and every shoddy canvas fails.
Well here is Shakespeare back in Avon,
wordless and broke. Art's not all you'd hoped.

(Coda)

Then again, here's Whitman
still composing poems to the breeze
that cools his housebound flesh.
There's remedy yet.
Today you may not make a master-mistress piece:
so what? Pick up your brush.
Get back to work.

THE ALYSCAMPS (LEAF-FALL)

Don't show me Autumn yet.
Where I am it's another flooded summer –
endless falling water and the sheep's hooves
rotting in the sodden fields.
This fever's got me blubbering in bed,
twisting tissues and afraid.
I'm thinking of the trees, how they age so fast –
it's already June and the leaves are black
with chlorophyll when moments ago
they were just a light green mist,
a sort of haar about the branches.
All this push to get out the green,
to seed before they sleep – six months
hectic, six months halfway dead,
traumatised and starved – do they ever get
a message back – in the pollen say,
of saplings, generation? Don't tell me
trees don't think like that. They know more
than you of give and take, of sharing light,
their slow accommodations, whole forests
on the move –

Forgive me.
I'm sick of the endless treadmill of fever
and this lethargy beneath it all,
its constant undertow. Summer's
halfway done and there's not been enough
to set in store. You won't come home
this winter or the next. I'll put the kettle on
and light the lamps in every room,
and this house will sail into the cold
like some droll ship, with me the drunkard
out on deck lashed to the leaf-stripped mast
and weeping, I'm so afraid of drowning,

while all the hoar-winds have to sing
is how tired I am, how very tired and leaden.
If I could only keep some sweetness
from the woods – honeycomb,
the trees' tapped sugar – some bright show,
some overwhelming colour: love,
come blaze, burn through the dark forever.

It's gold under the awning. No longer summer,
but café lamps incinerate the dark
and all its gold internal doors lead into warmth.
High blue shutters open on the street,
a tree drips needles on the cobblestones,
shop-fronts doze. A night like this is good for living.
You can hear the kiss of lips leaving a cigarette,
a couple making love upstairs, the wild stars
spinning . . . You paint a broken yolk of gold
as quickly as you can and the café dais
goes on and on, the garçon waiting cock-a-hip
for the last late-flirters – brandy-talkers,
mean with tips and slow to drink,
wrapped up warm; in it for the long haul.

WHEATFIELDS, WILD HORSES

wind whitens the grass
like wild herds riding the Camargue
and in a far field
the shadow of a cloud

SALVAGE

Dawn floods through
the valley from the east.
A feral rose

grown up
through the thorn bush
is caught in its currents –

a single bloom transformed,
become its own lantern
hung above the garden,

radiant, elect,
its ventricles and channels
charged with light,

its scarlet bell streaming,
as if it were Christ's sacred heart
radiating flames,

spilling at the brim
with the jewel-bright pulse
of morning,

already beginning to break apart
with a love of the world
beyond limit, or bearing.

POEM FOR JAMES

Summer; thunder pulsed on the horizon
while hummingbirds slipped through the thickened air
to circle the dropper, sip sugared water,
and I half-waded, half-swam, thigh-deep in pollen,
which rose in a haze from their meadow-grown lawn.
I was straight off the bus in that glaze of heat,
my unwashed skin peppery with sweat,
rucksack, camera, dirt, bearing me down
to the devil. But there you were, waist-deep in saffron,
your long arms folded and every hair on them
glowing like bronze, your red hair on fire
and your dark eyes attentive, though you don't remember,
which is why I'm writing it down, from the goldenrod in bloom
to your nimbus of insects lit by the sun.

ZITHERIXON IDOL

You slept at the root of the black oak tree,
the back of your head erupted in sap,
a blistering of resin beads.

What about the one who made you,
chapped and split the rude heart-wood,
fashioned your neck and its wattle of bark,

the palms-weight of your balls, your perfect
upright cock, your helmet and beard?
Out near the clay-works leaves unpack

stiff lobes and the pinprick nub
of the pink oak-flower pushes clean.
From the smallest speck these green roosts come,

their storeys of lichen and spunk, brash
for the fire. How did you answer her
greenwood god, marsh-water oar?

Is there anyone among us now
to carry her trace, the swerve of her instep,
the beautiful glint of her hair?

PRAYER

I saw you like a hare, stripped and jugged
in your own blood, your tail a rudder
steering you through burgundy and juniper,
your eyes gummed shut. Tadpole,

stripling, elver, don't let the dragtides
pull you under, but root in, bed down,
tucked behind my pelvic bone,
rocked in the emptying stoup of my womb.

SHEEP

She's lying under a low wind
bedded in mud and afterbirth,
her three dead lambs

knotted in a plastic bag.
Crows have pecked out her arse
and now the hen

that's been circling all morning
tugs at a string of birth-meat
like she's pulling a worm in the yard.

I can't not watch.
I too lay stunned
in my own dirt,

the miscarried child
guttering out,
soaking the mattress in blood.

I was afraid to look down
for what I might see –
a human face, a fist.

Yet once it was done I got up,
gathered my bedding
and walked.

The sky's locked down. I've left the shell of myself
curled up on the quilt in her own penumbra of dark,
too far gone to weep. Dog has also sloughed
the shadow of her sleeping double and barrels
up the path, through gold-spun meadows spliced
with flowers to a stile knee-deep in thistle-drift.
We've come up here to breathe. It is a sort of high
rope bridge: look how the valley sways
with its weight of traffic and discontent.
There is our house. My work in pieces on the desk.
Dog has vectored rabbit spoor and will not wait;
the slipped jewels of rain and grass-seed spray
from her coat as she drags me up above
the level of the cloud-break. Pigeons scare
then wheel away while we still stand,
faltered by the light, landlocked, hide-bound.

TOBOGGAN RUN

Midnight, early February. Moonlight – trapped
between the snow still falling and the white earth –
is luminous from our sloped roof to the firs
that edge the common land. In the white curve

of the field beyond, figures almost drowned
in the static interference of snow and distance
toboggan down the spills. They're so far off,
so dimly seen – a black speck riding the cataracts

and screes of our deepest snowfall in years.
Their runners leave the snow-warp as they leap,
like animals possessed beyond their strength –
spawning salmon, startled deer. What would I give

to be one of those swimmers in all this snow,
swallowed by the cold and the night's strange radiance?
Would I leave this house, its synthesis of brightness,
would I give myself to the wind? The snow pulls a veil

across the moonlit world, deepens and draws in
on figures lost to the year's last blizzard,
tobogganing a swerving run through our rarest weather,
on and on, liturgy or evensong or requiem for snow.

LARES

I keep going back to that bird, snagged
by a halter or skein of fibre or yarn
and strung from the gutter of the opposite house
where it quartered the wind, each bead of its spine
and the dead-drop of its skull
lit up against the breeze-block wall,
claws pushed out as if skidding to a halt
while its beak transmitted code.

I say a prayer to you, small ghost,
small noosed spirit of the eaves,
dangling from the prow of the house
singing all four winds, the spindle and pin
and needle and thorn of your hollow bones
riding you on air that is redolent with spores
after the fact of your scavenged heart,
the stolen tissues of your wings.

SOUNDINGS

There's a leveret in the field.
I know it by its mother's haunt at dusk,
can sense the cupped space of its watch
over near the gorse.

For now it's stowed
belly to the thawed ground, screened
in timothy and vetch, tuned
to the wing-chirr of insects,

the far-off bark of a fox.
As for you, small one in my womb,
the midwife lies an ear down flat
to hear the wild, sweet beating

of your heart,
scans for tell-tale movements on the graph.
There are still so many ways
you could startle, abort.

BREW

Hunched genie in the lamp of my womb
taking on bone till your spine glows
like a flexed wand, multiplying cells
like pearls.

Self-contained, remote,
a kernel in a walnut shell
you're that well-sealed, all voltage and will,
a knotted concentration in the dark,

feather and tar,
meconium and fur –
your fingers bud and clot;
blood roars to your spendthrift heart.

CHILDBED

I looked and saw,
collared in my own dark fur,
your face, blurry with vernix, strange,

like a drawing by the Master
pen and ink over wet chalk
and pricked for transfer.

Out you slid, cabled and wet,
delivered, time of birth given;
yet what I keep is that first look

at your pause half-born, sheathed
from the neck down, crowned
in unfamiliar regions of light and air,

your lungs beginning to draw
as you verged on our world
and waited, prescient, rare.

REPAIRS

D'you mind the midwife
sitting on a stool
between my stirruped legs
and putting on her specs

like a goodly house-bess
with a reading lamp
and her work
in her lap . . .

It must be the gas
that has me see her
holding pins
between her tightened lips

as she works
with both hands
round the wound
to stitch me back in.

MILK FEVER

When she screams
I can't help it,
I sweat and the skin
of my nipples becomes

like water's skin,
that thin meniscus
I've seen dimple and crease
round a pond-skater's feet –

think of the way water
begins to tremble
in its glass
as the earthquake begins –

so my breasts pulse
and the fine membrane
of each nipple
tightens,

lets through
a drop of milk –
she calls to my body
and my body leaps.

BREASTFEEDING

i

But really it's like this –
weeping as your milk comes in,
clutching a hot poultice
and counting through the pain
as you bring her on
to the hardened breast.

There's a whole new grammar
of tongue-tie and latch –
the watery foremilk
with its high acid content,
the fatty hindmilk
that separates in the fridge

to a thick skim
at the top of the flask,
and the nursing bra
like a complex lock
as you fumble, one-handed
at the catch.

She has a stomach
the size of a marble
and feeds in and out
of days.

You are lost
to the manifold
stations of milk,
the breast siphoned off

then filling,
yellow curd
of the baby's shit
you get down on your knees

at the foot of the change-mat
to clean,
holding your breath.
It was always like this;

a long line of women
sitting and kneeling,
out of their skins
with love and exhaustion.

COUNCIL OFFICES

The registrar asks
if this is our *first*
live-born child;

and I think
of the shuttered room
and rolling screen –

my empty womb
and that failed scrap
of foetal sac –

then remember again
the corridor
of the labour ward

and that woman
sitting weeping
with her man

having given birth
to a death –
small grey face,

no breath,
something you cannot help
but love –

habibi, akushla,
I go home alone
but carry you,

courie you,
little slipped thing,
to the ends of the earth.

VISITATIONS

She stares
over my left shoulder
into blank corners

and seems to watch
who knows what
bright travellers.

Wring out the room,
make it clean.
I'll have no ministers,

no auspices –
she's not your passenger
or plaything,

not your holy fool;
back off.
Leave us be.

CRADLE CAP

It begins as a roughness,
then spreads to a lichenous crust
that helmets your head for months,
and for months a cuckoo-spit salve
wets down your scalp
as we try to soak it off.

At last it lifts
bringing out your hair in tufts
till you look for all the world
like my own, small, robin-in-the-moult
with your dishevelled feathers,
stuck quills.

Little hedge familiar,
you came to us perfect;
now you claw at your head
and draw blood, till your skull
is as scritch-scratched and scored
as if we'd left you to sleep in the gorse.

Yet this is what we hope for,
that you roughen, weather –
darling, you cannot always be this tender,
but hush you and heal
and soon you'll come fledging into this life
tempered and whole.

TENTSMUIR

The Arctic Terns are back.
They come for the light,
chasing summertime
from the Antarctic to here,

addicted to brightness
that drags at the throat
and never lets fall,
while all the while

Winter's stain
chases at their heels.
I watch one with its black eyes
like the puncture of a snakebite

scanning for fish.
It snatches at the water
then draws back, scalded
by loneliness that haunts there.

DEMETER

Up in shorn Drake's Meadow the hay bales shine.
They're sheathed in plastic tubing, and the plastic
is slack at each end then tight round the bale
like a film. My daughter is compelled –
she must fit her arms round each bale, or pull
at their silver tails and I cannot draw her home.
I head down the path hoping she'll come
but when I look back she's gone and my own voice
snags at her name like barbed wire on skin.
When I see her again she's halfway down the field
emerging from behind another bale
as if they were portals or wormholes to pass her
through this sun-bleached meadow – impossible –
her mouth is bruised with blackberry juice
and she keeps disappearing, the way a cormorant
will dive, then reappear a mile upriver,
disappearing, as if into hell through the shadow
of a hay bale – Demeter will be screaming soon,
cutting her wrists with broken glass,
rubbing in dirt, turning the world to darkness and ice
she misses her daughter so much (pathological) –
black ice on the school run, shuddering cars,
bodies through glass – she can't bear it and I
can't stand it – not that small smashed body on the road
nor the germs – septicaemia, meningitis –
her small blotched body in my arms –
nor the men preparing underground rooms –
bare mattress and a bucket, concealed stairs –
what mother could find you there,
digging up the pavement with her nails –
I can't bear it and I cannot pray enough
to spare it, I'll pray to any listening god
to keep her safe from harm, I go and pick
my daughter up and carry her protesting home.

PINE CONE

Look at the long
wooden petals
of the cone,

each splayed latch
keeled like a boat
and riderless,

the seeds utterly sprung.
I hold the damp weight
of the cone in my palm

and think about the saplings –
where they've rooted
and how far gone

till I can see the acid green
of their needles
soft as hair,

vulnerable to clearances
and the long blunt teeth
of the deer.

One day
my daughter also
will travel far from here.

SMALL MERCIES

After James Schuyler

A rare summer day;
the wisteria is sending out
its young green whips
and beyond it is a spruce –
its yieldings and cobweb runs,
its holdings of resin and dust.
Outside a cricket is chirping –
maybe it's the same cricket
I just turfed out of the room,
caught in a makeshift trap.
The cricket raised itself
on its strong back haunches
like some kind of centaur
and pawed at the glass
with its whiskery front legs;
and once I'd gone down
to the garden
and tipped it out on the grass
it looked a little stunned
and wheeled round and round
like the misguided needle
of a drunken compass.
It was brown as the earth.
And I thought maybe it was done for,
that it'd been indoors too long
and was slowing down.
But now I think I hear it chirping
and perhaps another cricket answering;
some children are jumping
on a trampoline
and the sound of rusty springs
may even be drawing it to song

and I am grateful to have set
one prisoner free
to sex and generation.
And now I find myself
wondering why I'm here –
James is off work
and pottering in the garden,
bagging up weeds
our daughter's at the park
with a friend –
why haven't we gone
to the meadows for a walk
why aren't we making love
why aren't we anywhere
but at our responsible work –
James weeding in the tangled beds
and me indoors with my book
in this cool study room
looking out,
partly longing to be free
and partly unable to wish myself
anywhere but here
with the good sound of James
sweeping up the leaves
and my pen moving across the page
and the occasional cricket
calling, calling
to love in another garden,
the marvellous elsewhere.

RIVER, SECOND MISCARRIAGE

I'd seen you before,
a half-formed soul
trailing caul
like a comforter,

then there you were –
detritus snagged
in the river's curve,
bottlenecked and beached

yet more than gone –
a wet clump
the specialist extracts
with a speculum and forceps

so I can run on,
raked clean.
Where, then, should I go
but here –

where water-light falls
down the shore wall
and small birds
glean in the mud

with their delicate bills
and the tide
comes and goes
like breathing.

You knew you'd find me
at the river's mouth,
you knew
that I'd be weeping.

FOETAL POLE

Same remnants on the scan –
the small, spoilt yolk
of the embryo sac

and this thin white line –
a hair picked from the sleeve of a coat,
faint blueprint of a spine.

ROSEBAY WILLOWHERB

September: the chirp of crickets rises
                from the harvested hayfield.
                        like a question, like a small self-doubt.

I'm stumbling into a bad pause –
                help me find the words:
                        something of happiness, for once –

of my daughter pretending to snore in my lap
                after stories at night
                        so I won't put her down in her cot,

or holding on to my leg to steady herself
                as she pinches off berries
                        and pushes them into her mouth;

or something of these fields themselves,
                the middle ditch lush
                        with brambles and sloes.

I too may be taking root,
                lit like this willowherb steeple
                        disrobing itself in the sun,

its long, unravelling hank of down
                wadded like cotton-wool,
                        its candelabra-d arms

spent and beautiful. The breeze lifts
                and the meadow is flying
                        with seed-threads.

My fledgling daughter is hanging round my knees,
her hair is the same white gold
as the white gold seeds

and here is the quick of the thing –
all my heart's stitches
for this new, bright being.

DAUGHTER SONG

for Isla

once all this is done –
soaping you in the bath
your half-songs and wet arms
and the owl in the woods behind the house
and the scream of a vole caught up
soaring through the boundless dark

and once all this is gone –
the sea crept in from the dazzling bay
its mouth even now at the red cliffs
once it's travelled in
and these high meadows are under water entirely
the vetch rotted back

and the warrens flooded sumps
and the fox runs trampled by the current
and the fox herself long drowned
still my love for you will ride, ride on
like that star in the old songs
its long-journeyed light

helpless and absolute
yes, though it makes no sense –
and I speak for your father also in this –
our love is like that
it hurtles on and on
and you are its lodestone
and you are the ground it falls upon

NOTES & ACKNOWLEDGEMENTS

DUMNONIA: the six poems in this series, commissioned by Wordquest/ Aune Head Arts, take various places in Devon as their stepping-off points. These are: Westward Ho! ('Submerged Forest'), Kent's Cavern, Torquay ('Cave Bear'), Postbridge, Dartmoor ('Clapper Bridge'), St Michael's Parish Church, Ashburton ('Urn-Burial'), Rougemont Castle, Exeter ('Rougemont') and HMNB Devonport ('Devonport'). 'Devonport' is dedicated to my father, David Benson. 'Rougemont' is dedicated to Temperance Lloyd, who was one of the three last people to be executed for alleged witchcraft in England. Temperance Lloyd, Susannah Edwards and Mary Trembles were held and tried at Rougemont Castle, before being hung at the Magdalen Drop (now a car park); Temperance Lloyd is believed to have been around eighty years old. The Dumnonia sequence as a whole is arranged chronologically, and 'Dumnonia' itself is a name for dark-age Devon and some of its surrounding areas.

'Emmaus' – the title of this poem concerns the appearance of Christ in the gospels of Saint Mark (16:12) and Saint Luke (24:13). In the gospel of Saint Luke 'two of them' were walking to Emmaus when 'Jesus himself drew near, and went with them. But their eyes were holden that they should not know him.' (24:15–16) The two invite Jesus to share supper with them, and as he breaks bread 'their eyes were opened, and they knew him; and he vanished out of their sight.' (Luke 24:31) This seemed to resonate with the way the elemental world might perceive humans – brief mortals, here then gone.

LOVE-LETTER TO VINCENT: each of the poems in 'Love-Letter to Vincent' take as their stepping-off point Van Gogh's own painting titles. Both the painting titles and the opening quotation are taken from Leo Jansen, Hans Luijten and Nienke Bakker (eds), *Vincent Van*

69

Gogh – The Letters: The Complete Illustrated and Annotated Edition (Thames and Hudson Ltd, London: 2009).

'Zitherixon Idol': the Zitherixon Idol, also known as the Kingsteignton Figure, was found in the Zitherixon ball-clay quarry near Kingsteignton in 1867 and has been radiocarbon dated to 426–352 BC. The Zitherixon Idol is unusual amongst such figures in being symmetrical and clearly male. It may have been a child's toy or, as the poem suggests, a fertility symbol or god. It is currently housed in the Royal Albert Memorial Museum in Exeter.

'Tentsmuir': Tentsmuir is the name of a nature reserve (Tentsmuir Forest and Kinshaldy Beach) on the East Coast of Fife, just north of St Andrews.

'Pine Cone' is dedicated to my mother, Jane Benson.

Thanks and acknowledgements are due to the editors of the following publications, where some of these poems have appeared: *Addicted to Brightness, Areté, Faber New Poets 1, Granta, Granta Online, IN Magazine, London Review of Books, New Statesman, Poetry London, Poetry Review, Silk Road Review, Tender* and *The Times Literary Supplement*, also to the editors and producers of BBC Radio Three's *Poetry Proms* which broadcast some of these poems in Summer 2012. 'Dumnonia' was commissioned by Wordquest Devon (Aune Head Arts) and Cyprus Well (Literature Works South West).

I am grateful to the Arts Council for a 'Grants for the Arts' Award

With thanks to John Burnside, Julia Copus, Douglas Dunn, Peter Straus and the wonderful Mincing Poets for their encouragement and support and to Frances Leviston, Robin Robertson and David-Antoine Williams for their advice and close reading of this manuscript. Thanks and love as always to my husband James Meredith and our daughter Isla.